The Industrial Revolution: Changes and Challenges

Reader

Core Knowledge®

Copyright © 2018 Core Knowledge Foundation
www.coreknowledge.org

All Rights Reserved.

Core Knowledge®, Core Knowledge Curriculum Series™,
Core Knowledge History and Geography™ and CKHG™
are trademarks of the Core Knowledge Foundation.

Trademarks and trade names are shown in this book
strictly for illustrative and educational purposes and are
the property of their respective owners. References herein
should not be regarded as affecting the validity of said
trademarks and trade names.

ISBN: 978-1-68380-334-8

The Industrial Revolution: Changes and Challenges

Table of Contents

The Industrial Revolution: Changes and Challenges
Reader
Core Knowledge History and Geography™

Chapter 1
Effects of the Industrial Revolution

The World Transformed Some of the most important changes in all of human history began in Great Britain in the 1700s and early 1800s.

During those years, steam-powered engines and pumps began to replace animals and human muscle power. Steam engines helped pump water out of coal mines. They helped grind grain into flour. They ran machines in factories that powered **looms** to weave cotton or woolen cloth.

The Big Question

How would you describe working conditions in the early part of the Industrial Revolution?

Vocabulary

loom, n. a machine used to weave threads into cloth

More and more, factories became a familiar sight across a landscape that had once been largely agricultural.

As the **Industrial Revolution** gained speed, factories sprang up in one city after another. These factories drew many workers from the countryside to the cities. Thousands of people who had lived according to the age-old rhythms of planting and harvesting began to live according to the new rhythms of the modern factory.

> **Vocabulary**
>
> **Industrial Revolution,** n. a period of history during which the use of machines to produce goods changed society and the economy
>
> **industrialization,** n. a shift to the widespread use of machines and factories to produce goods

By the late 1800s, the Industrial Revolution had spread beyond Great Britain. It had spread across the body of water called the English Channel to Europe and across the Atlantic Ocean to the United States. It had also begun to enter a new phase of development. Great Britain had taken the lead during the first phase of the Industrial Revolution, which featured steam power, coal, and cotton manufacturing. During the second phase, which featured steel, electricity, oil, and gas, the United States took the lead.

Like most great changes in human history, the Industrial Revolution has had positive and negative results. Generally speaking, the Industrial Revolution improved the lives of millions by making a great variety of goods more affordable and more widely available. Most importantly though, the Industrial Revolution provided new kinds of employment opportunities for people.

But **industrialization** has also had less desirable consequences. For instance, it has led to great inequalities of wealth. Almost from the beginning, factory owners and businessmen became very wealthy, while most workers toiled away in factories and generally remained poor. The workers who lived through the early phases of the Industrial Revolution had an especially hard time. These workers worked long hours in dangerous circumstances. They received low wages and had little or no legal protection. And, industrialization has had a significant impact on our environment, too!

Quite often, men, women, and children worked all day in factories for very little money.

Historians have many records of what it was like to live in Great Britain during the early stages of the Industrial Revolution. We can read, for example, about Patience Kershaw, a girl who worked in the coal mines near Manchester, England, in the 1840s. Here is a part of her story.

Patience Kershaw Speaks Out

"When they ask you a question, Patience Kershaw, look them right in the eye and tell the truth. That's all they want, the truth. You are doing this for your father, may he rest in peace. And for your sisters and your brothers. It is for our family, Patience. We can't go on like this."

"Yes, Mother."

Patience wanted to do just as her mother asked. But when she stood before the gentlemen from London—a Parliamentary Committee of Inquiry—and tried to answer their questions, she began to tremble. She worried that they would laugh at her ragged pants and jacket, and especially at her bare feet. She wished she had a dress. Even though she had washed herself that morning, she still felt dirty. Coal dust was caked around her eyes and in her hair. Her hands were bruised and sore. She looked worn and old.

Lord Ashley himself asked her how old she was.

"Seventeen, sir."

When he smiled and softly said he had a daughter just about her age, Patience realized these men meant her no harm. Their questions about her life and work in the coal mines were not meant to make fun of her, Lord Ashley said. Patience took a deep breath.

She told them that her father had died in a mining accident. She was the oldest of ten children. Her three sisters worked in the mill, but she and six brothers worked in the mine. Her youngest brother was five.

"He works, too?"

"Yes, sir. We all work."

"And school?"

"No, sir, I never went to school. I cannot read or write. None of us Kershaws can."

"Tell us about your work, Patience."

"I go [into the mine] at five o'clock in the morning and come out at five in the evening. I get my breakfast of porridge and milk first; I take my dinner with me, a cake [a thick, oat cracker] and I eat as I go; I do not stop or rest any time."

"Twelve hours each day?"

"Yes, sir. I have to walk about a half-hour to get to work, so I am up early. And home late, long after dark. I don't mind in the summer, but it's raw in the winter, and the rain."

"What clothes do you have?"

"I [work] in the clothes I have now on."

Lord Ashley looked at the other men, especially the doctor. He frowned and wrote something down in a large book that was open on the table in front of him.

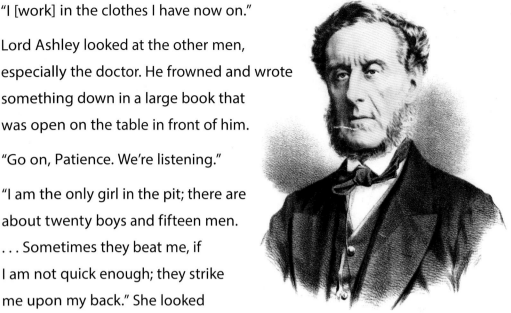
Lord Ashley

"Go on, Patience. We're listening."

"I am the only girl in the pit; there are about twenty boys and fifteen men. . . . Sometimes they beat me, if I am not quick enough; they strike me upon my back." She looked down at her feet and began to sob.

"I would rather work in the mill than in the coal-pit." She started to cry even louder now.

"Thank you, Patience. You may go."

Child Labor

When Patience Kershaw left the room, Lord Ashley spoke to the members of the committee: "Imagine, gentlemen! This, in the year of our Lord 1842. Our beloved Queen Victoria herself is just a few years older than this poor girl. We must do something to prevent the sons and daughters of this nation from the excess zeal of our industrialists. We must act in Parliament."

Lord Ashley had summoned Patience Kershaw to testify about one of the great problems created by the Industrial Revolution: the problem of child labor. Thousands of children, many of them younger than you are, worked in the mines and in the factories during the early stages of the Industrial Revolution. They had to. Their parents needed every penny of income to care for their large families, especially when they could not find work themselves.

The owners of factories and mines actually preferred children over adult laborers. Children worked in small, cramped quarters. They could and would be beaten if they disobeyed. They often did dangerous tasks that adults would refuse to do. Above all, they were easily replaced. There were always more children looking for work. Many orphanages gladly contracted out their children to bring the owners some profit. Families that were sent to the **poorhouse** because they could not pay their rent or other bills often had no choice but to send their children to work. If the father of a family lost his job or was injured or died, the mother and her children were desperate. They had to beg or work, and often did both.

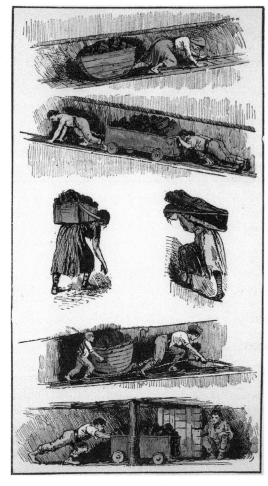

Children were employed in mines and in factories. They could work in small, cramped places and were easily replaced. There were no laws to protect working children at the start of the Industrial Revolution.

Changes for Everyone

Gradually, reformers, or people who wanted to change things for the better in Great Britain and in other European countries, passed laws to protect women and children from harsh and unsafe working conditions. Inspectors traveled to factories and mines; small children were required to attend school at least two hours a day. These measures,

Vocabulary

poorhouse, n. a place where poor people were sent to live if they were unable to pay their bills

when they were enforced, certainly helped. But working men were still at the mercy of employers. Becoming ill or getting fired could happen at any time. Horrible poverty and suffering could still befall whole towns and country areas if prices fell. What kept the workers going was, at times, the promise of a better life.

Many people looked to America as the place where that new life might begin. People heard stories that there was gold in the streets, just waiting to be picked up! This made many want to leave the lands where their families had lived for centuries.

Still other workers in Great Britain and in Europe wanted to stay and improve things at home. They wanted more sweeping reforms, even a revolution that would free them from an economic system that seemed merciless. When they formed **unions** and refused to work in such bad conditions, they were sometimes arrested and sent to jail. Often, they would never work again.

> **Vocabulary**
>
> **union,** n. an organization formed by workers to win and protect workers' rights
>
> **economy,** n. the way a country manages its money and resources to produce, buy, and sell goods and services

The Industrialists

Workers weren't the only ones to complain. Many factory and mine owners were unhappy, too. They believed that many of the laws introduced to protect the workers were unfair, and that working conditions were really not that bad. Many argued that the government had no right to interfere in the free exchange of goods and labor. The pay might be low, and the work at times dangerous, but no one was actually forcing people to do it. After all, people chose to work in factories or in mines.

These industrialists believed that the **economy** would balance, or take care of itself naturally, if left alone. No one would supply or produce more goods than could be sold at a fair price; and no one would want goods that were too expensive or undesirable. If the government interfered too much, it would upset this balance, they argued. For example, if the government stepped in to set conditions for workers' safety or for the quality or amount of goods being produced, the employers' profits would be affected. This, in turn, would affect the price of the goods and the wages paid to the worker. In the end, there would be no **free market**, and perhaps fewer jobs too! Everyone would be worse off. In their minds, the factory owners were doing the right thing.

Vocabulary

free market, n. an economic system based on competition between private businesses, where the government does not control prices

Industrialists argued that by being forced to make factories and mines safer and healthier they would make less money and this could reduce workers' wages. Generally though, their main concern was keeping their profits as high as possible.

Of course, many of these industrialists' idea of a "free market" meant that they should be free to make as much money as they could. They saw anyone who argued to the contrary as an enemy of business. Because they were wealthy and had great influence in society, these men often held political power or could influence those who did. Thankfully, there were some outstanding exceptions, such as the determined Lord Ashley. But for the most part, many wealthy industrialists disliked those who sought to change things. They did what they could to strengthen their grasp on their wealth and privilege, or at least to stall any reforms. Meanwhile, the Patience Kershaws and her brothers and sisters of the era suffered.

Chapter 2
Before the Industrial Revolution

Old Ways To understand how the Industrial Revolution changed people's lives, we need to know what life was like before it began. That means learning a little about agricultural life in England— a part of Great Britain—in the 1600s and 1700s.

The Big Question

What was rural life like for ordinary people before the Industrial Revolution?

This image shows serfs at work in medieval England. Serfdom began to die out in England after the Peasants' Revolt of 1381.

Serfdom disappeared from England during the 1400s. **Serfs** became villagers. These villagers were no longer tied to the land in the way that serfs had been. They rented land and were free to move if another **landlord** offered them better terms. Some villagers even became prosperous **yeomen** farmers. Some of them hired other villagers as farm workers, and a few were even accepted as **gentry**—members of the landholding elite. But most rural English people were very poor. Sometimes groups of people moved about searching for work. If they were lucky, they either found work as hired farm workers or rented humble cottages and garden plots.

A Hard Life

Patience Kershaw's distant ancestors, like almost all English people of that earlier time, worked from sunrise to sunset in fields near their village or town. They used windmills and waterwheels to help them grind grain or pump water out of flooded fields; they used oxen in the fields. Poorer people, however, had to use their own muscle power. Everyone faced the same problem: producing enough food to survive. A lot depended on the weather. The rest depended on everyone's hard work.

When the weather was good, farmers grew wheat, rye, barley, and oats. They took these grains to nearby mills to be ground into flour. They baked the flour into bread or ate it as a mush or porridge. If there was enough grain, the farmers would also feed grain to their livestock.

Vocabulary

serfdom, n. an agricultural system in which people (serfs) were not free, but were required to stay and work for a landowner as the owner demanded

serf, n. a peasant who is not free; a person living on a feudal estate who was required to work for the lord of the manor

landlord, n. a person who owns property that other people pay to use or live in

yeoman, n. a person who owns and works on a small farm

gentry, n. people who own land and have high social standing but no titles of nobility

Medieval villages were usually centered around a church and a mill. There might also be a large house belonging to a lord or a rich family. There was usually a river nearby also.

Patience Kershaw's ancestors also grew vegetables and herbs in their gardens. They might get eggs from their chickens, ducks, or geese. Some were lucky enough to have apple or pear trees or to find wild berries. Others might catch fish in a nearby pond or river. Yeomen farmers might make cheese from their goats' or cows' milk or yarn from their sheep's wool. Whatever was extra could be sold or traded at the market.

Every village and town had at least one market every week or so during the warmer months. Villagers could get items they needed or wanted but might not be able to produce themselves: salt, spices, perhaps a mirror or a bit of fancy cloth, or a comb carved from tortoise shell. Having something special, then as now, made people feel happy.

The Seasons

In winter, poor villagers would have to slaughter their pigs, sheep, ducks, geese, and chickens rather than try to feed them until the next year's grain could be harvested. Come spring, they would probably trade something they made—perhaps a knit sweater, a woven blanket, or carved wooden spoons—for a piglet or a lamb, or baby ducks, geese, and chicks.

Each spring, farm workers had to plow and smooth the fields. If the fields were too wet, the wooden plow might get stuck; if the fields were too dry, the plow might break. If there was no team of oxen or horses or even a cow, the farmers had to push or pull the plow down the field themselves. Even small children had to help in the fields and at home.

Vocabulary
....
poach, v. to hunt or fish illegally

Seed was precious. If the spring rains didn't come at just the right time, the seedlings died in the fields. Crows were constant pests—mice and rats, too. Foxes preyed on the geese, ducks, and chickens. To make matters worse, villagers were not allowed to hunt the deer or rabbits that ate their crops. The lord reserved this pastime for himself and his family. Many a villager was punished harshly for **poaching** the lord's game.

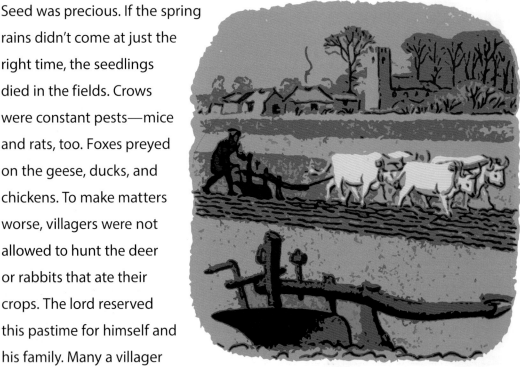

Tending to the fields, as well as planting and harvesting, were very important jobs for farmers. It was essential that their crops grew.

The Harvest

Men usually harvested the grain by going down the rows on their knees and swinging a short, curved blade called a sickle. If they had a scythe—a longer curved blade mounted on a long handle—they could stand up as they moved down the rows and cut the stalks. Then, the farmers had to dry and bundle the stalks, take them to barns, and thresh, or beat them until the edible grain was freed from the husks.

Animals could eat the grain at this point. But if the wheat or rye was going to be made into flour and baked, a farmer would have to take it to the mill. Of course, he had to

Harvesting grain was hard work, and it was all done by hand, using a scythe. The use of the scythe continued for hundreds of years—even into the 1800s and early 1900s.

be careful to save some seed grain for the next year's crop. Many families worried through the winter that they would not have enough food to last them until the next harvest, several months away.

Rural life was governed by the seasons, each in turn bringing its chores and celebrations. But everything depended on the success of the harvest. Starvation might have been rare, but **malnutrition** was common among the working poor. Malnutrition

> **Vocabulary**
>
> **malnutrition,** n. a state of poor health due to not having enough healthy food

opened the door to sickness and disease. Diseases that we no longer consider deadly, such as measles, whooping cough, and chicken pox, were often fatal.

Medical practices depended on home remedies based on herbs and prayers. Life may have been predictable, but it was rarely easy.

Daily Life Before Modern Times

Most village houses had one large room with a low ceiling and a dirt floor. An open hole in the roof let out the smoke from the fireplace but let in the rain and snow. There was very little furniture. Most homes probably had a rough table and a few benches, made by the residents themselves. Beds were little more than sacks of straw. The whole family often slept together to stay warm. The toilet was usually a hole in the ground outside. A barrel near the hut might collect rainwater, but more often than not, several families in the village used a common well or a nearby stream or pond to get water.

There were no schools or hospitals. Almost no one could read or write. The priest was usually the only educated person in the village. The largest building in the village or town was usually a church. Roads were often mere muddy ruts.

The local lord or yeoman farmer hired villagers as dayworkers to help him build his manor house, tend his gardens and orchards, or mend his roads and walls. Women often worked in the lord's or farmer's house. They did laundry or other household chores. Children might be put in charge of herding flocks of geese or chasing crows from gardens and fields.

Poor folks took work where they could find it to earn a bit of money to pay their rent or buy something in the market. Poor people were grateful to find work. What other choice did they have? They could hope for a better life for their children. But being born poor usually meant dying poor.

Having enough food to eat and staying warm and healthy were important concerns for poor farmers and villagers.

The Powerless Poor

The poor typically had no say in government nor any power to change their lives in a peaceable way. Protests were often put down with ruthless force. For most men, women, and children, life in this world may have often felt dreary and painful.

Patience Kershaw's ancestors who lived before the Industrial Revolution and modern times did not know any other life, of course. They did the best they could. Life did not seem to change much from year to year. But during the 1600s and 1700s, thanks to new technologies and important changes in farming, mining, and metal-making techniques, people's lives changed a great deal.

Chapter 3
Moving Toward the Industrial Age

New Ways of Farming If an English family living in, say, the 1300s could travel forward in time to the 1700s, they would notice that many things were still the same. But some important changes were happening.

The Big Question

In what ways did the inventions of the Industrial Revolution impact people's lives?

Before the Industrial Revolution, most people still worked on the land, struggling to put enough food on their table to keep from starving. Over the years, however, inventive people discovered new and more efficient ways to do their work. And foods, not known before, were brought across the Atlantic from the Americas. Potatoes grew well in moist, sandy English soil. Corn grew well, too, but most farmers thought it was only fit for farm animals! Most families probably never tasted chocolate; many never saw anyone smoking tobacco. These were expensive items and were only sampled by the wealthy.

Oxen, cows, horses, sheep, goats, and pigs were larger now, thanks to better feed and breeding practices. For many families, there was meat on the table more than just once or twice a year. Better-fed people were healthier and even noticeably taller than their ancestors. More sheep also meant more wool for clothing and blankets.

More important than the availability of new crops were the many new tools and farming techniques. New plows were stronger and heavier, and had metal blades.

An improved diet meant that people were healthier and even lived longer.

21

These plows allowed the plowman to loosen and turn over deeper, richer soil. Seedlings had better root systems and were less likely to dry out if there was little rain. New methods of harnessing **draft animals** made better use of their strength. Larger oxen or horses pulled these heavier plows more efficiently.

Agriculture was beginning to bring profits to the lords and some of the most enterprising villagers. Improved roads and newly dug canals made it easier for farmers to bring grain to the mill. Flour was more easily brought to markets in nearby towns, too. **Waterwheels** were improved, so mills could grind more flour. There was an enthusiasm for change, especially if it meant increased **productivity** and increased profit.

Vocabulary

"draft animal," (phrase) an animal used for pulling heavy loads

waterwheel, n. a wheel that is turned by flowing water and used to power machinery

productivity, n. the rate at which goods are made or work is completed

Waterwheels converted the power of flowing water into a form of energy that could power machinery. Often mills were built beside rivers and streams for this reason.

The Enclosure Movement

The English landscape began to change. Land where villagers had once grown crops was taken over by gentry landlords and "enclosed"—fenced in and turned into pasture for the sheep whose wool was in great demand for cloth. Meadows and woods that lords and villagers had shared were also enclosed. Previously the land was divided into many small plots. By the 1600s, larger, more efficient farms were emerging.

As this "enclosure movement" lumped together many small fields, the cost of producing crops fell. Fewer farm workers were needed. With bigger harvests and lower costs, the larger landlords reaped more profits and grew wealthier. But many villagers found themselves without work. Some hired themselves out as day laborers. Many rural families scraped together a modest living by doing weaving in their cottages. Desperate for work, hundreds of thousands of villagers had to leave the countryside, flocking to cities, to nearby mines, or to the American colonies. Eventually, these displaced people, and certainly their descendants, would become a large part of the labor force as the Industrial Age took hold.

New Ways of Mining and Making Metal Tools

By 1700, timber and firewood were scarce in England, and coal became an important source of energy. Coal could burn hot enough to soften iron. Iron was used to make new, stronger farm tools. It could also be used for strong bridges, and for machinery that would help dig canals and deepen harbors. Many wealthy English landowners began investing some of their profits in coal and iron mines.

Soon, the easy-to-mine coal and iron deposits that were close to the surface of the ground were used up. Miners dug **shafts** down underground to follow the minerals wherever they could. Quite often, these mines flooded with groundwater.

> **Vocabulary**
>
> **shaft,** n. a deep, narrow tunnel that gives access to a mine

Working underground in the mines was dangerous enough. But no one could work in a flooded mine. Something needed to be done to pump out the water. The power of steam was known to the ancient Greeks and Romans. They knew that when boiling water was confined in a sealed pot or drum, it could explode if the steam pressure was high enough. If, however, the steam was allowed to escape through a hole or a small tube, it produced a great force.

This is the principle behind a steam engine. By the early 1700s, several people began to devise steam pumps powered by coal fires. The early steam pumps were not very efficient. They were slow and too large to move around easily. Then, an observant and resourceful Scotsman named James Watt decided to improve on existing engines. The steam engine that Watt built in 1768 was smaller, more powerful, and more moveable than older engines. It was useful for pumping water out of mines. With improvements, by the 1780s Watt's engine also could run other machines through a system of gears, pulleys, and belts.

The steam engine pumped water out of coal mines making it easier, safer, and quicker to dig for coal.

Eventually, even smaller and more powerful steam engines would pull carts or wagons fitted onto rails. The first locomotive—Richard Trevithick's Portable Steam Engine—puffed along tracks in England in 1804. In the United States, Robert Fulton improved on earlier versions of a steam engine to drive a boat. In 1807, his *Clermont* steamed up the Hudson River from New York City to Albany. Other inventors adapted steam engines to machines that harvested wheat, spun thread, wove cloth, or lifted heavy hammers to forge iron.

Inventions and improvements could not be kept in one country. Anyone determined and clever enough could try their hand. There was some luck involved—and sometimes a great deal of fame and money for the successful inventor. The Industrial Revolution may have begun slowly, with improvements in growing crops. It really took off, however, when glowing coal melted iron ore or converted water to steam. With the production of iron, there were railroads and ships, bridges and barges, looms and machines of all kinds clanking and whirring, doing the work that once had been done by people and animals. It was a new age—the Industrial Age. Modern times had begun.

Almost every aspect of daily life was affected by the advancement of steam power. The fact that people could travel more easily, transport goods longer distances, and take advantage of new employment opportunities, had a profound effect on the way people lived.

Chapter 4
From Farms to Factories and Cities

Modern Urban Culture Today, we take big cities for granted. Even if we don't live in one, we know what they are like. Millions of people live in cities. There are busy streets filled with traffic and noise almost all the time. There are shops, stores, restaurants, and theaters in abundance—not to mention tall buildings. And in some cities there are factories, too! But about three hundred years ago, there were very few big cities. So what led to the fairly rapid rise of the modern city?

> ## The Big Question
>
> What developments in the manufacturing of cloth caused mass migration to industrial towns and cities?

Three or four hundred years ago, most people could not have imagined a city like New York City.

More People Than Ever Before

Between 1100 and 1300, Europe's population grew. Then, over the next two hundred years, it seems to have declined. Although many people were born, more were dying. Warfare, shortages of food, and disease were facts of life. During the **plagues** of the 1300s, as many as one third of all Europeans may have died.

Vocabulary

plague, n. a highly contagious, usually fatal, disease that affects large numbers of people

After 1500, however, the population began to grow again—although at times unevenly due to wars and outbreaks of diseases. We cannot be sure why, but it probably had to do with improved farming methods and more food. It also might have been because those who lived through the plague years developed some resistance to disease. And it might have been due to improved hygiene, or ways of keeping healthy and preventing disease.

Then, around 1700, Europe entered a phase of more rapid population growth. For example, over the next hundred years, Great Britain increased its population from five million to eight million. France grew at about the same pace. Other European populations increased between 60 and 80 percent.

In the 1700s, more and more people moved to towns and cities in search of jobs. The towns and cities became crowded, and at times, unhealthy places to live.

Europeans living in North America increased even more dramatically: from an estimated 275,000 in 1700 to nearly four million in 1790. Native Americans, however, tragically continued to decline in numbers, due to warfare and exposure to diseases brought across the Atlantic Ocean by Europeans.

We don't know exactly why the population of Europe began to grow quite so rapidly in the early 1700s. Whatever the causes may have been, at the same time, there were fewer jobs and therefore less work in the countryside. As agriculture became mechanized and more efficient, fewer people were needed for farming. The combination of more people and less need for farm workers drove many people out of the villages and into the cities. This massive **migration** from villages to cities is one of the most important historical events of the last millennium. It accounts for the growth of the modern industrial city.

It Started in England

Back in the year 1700, Patience Kershaw's great-great-great-grandfather might have gone from his village into the town of Manchester once or twice a year. At the market, he could trade one of his pigs for a woolen blanket or maybe an iron pot. At that time, Manchester was a rather large town, with about ten thousand inhabitants. Just 150 years later, around the time Patience was testifying to Lord Ashley's commission, more than three hundred thousand people lived and worked in Manchester.

The city had grown wildly, absorbing nearby villages and towns. It had become a hub of factories and commercial activities. **Barges** on a canal brought coal and iron to the city. In 1830, a railway linked it with Liverpool, one of the busiest harbors on England's Atlantic coast. From there, ships took Manchester's cloth to markets all around the world.

> ### Vocabulary
> ....
> **migration,** n. the act of moving from one place to another to live
>
> **barge,** n. a boat with a flat bottom, usually used for carrying goods

Changes in Cloth

Manchester was actually first known as a place where fine woolen cloth was woven. Later, it became the production center for a new kind of cloth, fustian (/fus*chun/). Fustian was a blend of linen and cotton

In the pre-industrial era, women often spun wool into thread at home, using a spinning wheel.

or wool. Fustian was sturdy and did not shrink as much as wool when it was washed. Before the industrial era, cloth making—from spinning, to dyeing, to weaving—was largely done by hand in the workers' homes.

Traditionally, women were hired to spin wool or cotton to produce yarn or thread. Men and women dyed the yarn or thread, but men were usually hired to do the weaving. Because so much depended on people working in their homes, the production of cloth was known as a cottage industry.

The Spinning Jenny

The Industrial Revolution changed all of this—not only for Manchester, but for other places, too. In the 1730s, John Kay invented the flying shuttle, which doubled the amount of cotton cloth that could be woven in any given day. The problem now was producing enough thread to keep up with the weavers. This

led to the invention of a machine known as a spinning jenny by James Hargreaves. Instead of one thread at a time, a jenny could spin several at once. However, this machine-spun thread was weak and often broke, making weaving a difficult process.

James Hargreaves's spinning jenny

The mule dramatically increased the production of thread. The cloth industry moved out of people's homes and into factories. Now the challenge was to produce enough cotton to send to the factories.

Then, in 1769, Richard Arkwright invented the water frame. It used water power at first, then steam, to drive rollers that stretched the thread before spinning it. This strengthened thread produced a tightly woven all-cotton fabric. Problem solved! By the end of 1700s, Samuel Crompton combined the jenny and the water frame into one large steam-driven machine, called a mule. This increased thread production by ten times. Larger and larger mules were built in special buildings, called factories. Cotton had also largely replaced wool. The problem now was growing enough cotton to keep up with the manufacturing process.

The Cotton Gin

An American named Eli Whitney knew that cotton grew well in the American South. But it wasn't easy to separate the cotton seeds from the fibers. In 1793, after studying the problem for just a few days, Whitney designed a simple machine that worked beautifully. Cotton was pushed through a hopper into contact with a revolving cylinder. Hundreds of wire hooks on the revolving cylinder strained out the seeds. Turning in the opposite direction, another cylinder combed or brushed the cotton off the hooks and into a bin. Whitney called his machine the cotton gin. *Gin* was short for engine.

The invention of the cotton gin meant the increased use of enslaved workers.

Whitney's invention changed agriculture in the American South. Huge cotton plantations developed, increasing demand for enslaved workers from Africa to produce "white gold," as cotton came to be known. The cotton gin made plantation owners and cotton merchants rich beyond their dreams.

The producers of cotton in the American South had an even greater financial advantage—their workers were enslaved and worked without receiving payment. The contribution of enslaved workers to the industrial development of the United States cannot be underestimated.

And sadly, because growing cotton was big business, Whitney's invention made slavery in America much less likely to disappear. Now there was enough cotton to keep the new factories—whether in Great Britain, or in the northern United States—working at full capacity.

Factories Instead of Cottages

There wasn't much difference between factories in Great Britain and those in the northern United States. Manufacturing techniques were very valuable. Workers had to swear not tell how the machinery worked. Spies tried to steal the secrets or bribe workers into revealing them. Most factory owners cared more for their profits than for their workers. To produce even more finished cloth, factories kept running after dark, with laborers working in shifts, by candle or lantern light.

Inside the factory, the owner and his overseers controlled the entire production process. Workers were under constant supervision and at the factory owner's mercy. He could pay a low wage, because so many people were looking for work. He would fire those who were uncooperative or unproductive. Children were especially cheap labor. Because they were small and quick, they could work in dangerous spots around the machinery.

And in Manchester, England, people soon said that the city was "steam mill mad." In 1830, it had ninety-nine cotton-spinning mills that worked from dawn to dark, making cotton cloth that found its way all around the world. Cloth made in a factory was superior in many ways, and it cost less than cloth made the old-fashioned way. By 1850, there were only 50,000 hand weavers in Britain, down from 250,000 just thirty years before. Parts of the quiet British countryside seemed to change almost overnight into huge, smoky, sooty, overcrowded cities.

Mining Areas in Great Britain

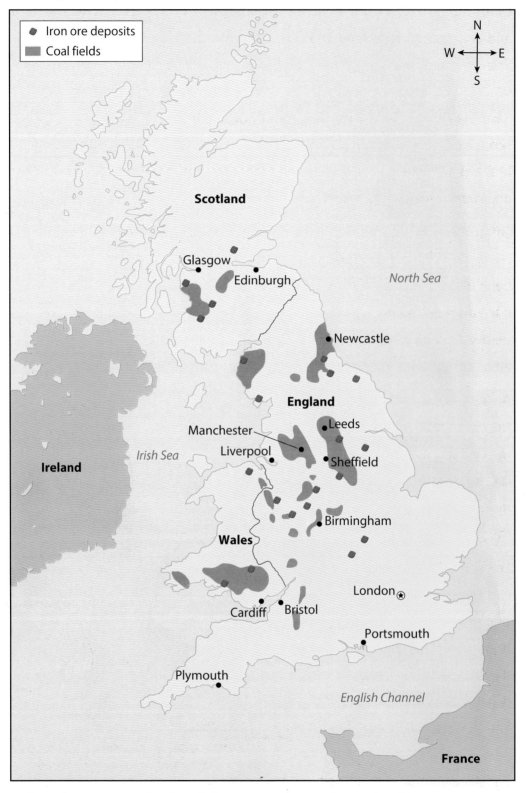

In the early 1800s, cities developed close to resources, such as coal and iron.

Families of workers flocked to these cities by the thousands. All hoped for a chance to earn a living and be better able to feed and clothe themselves than they had been back in their villages and small towns. Before moving to cities, they may not have known or been concerned about housing shortages, poor **sanitation**, and scarce food. Once in the city, however, there wasn't much they could do, except take work wherever they could find it.

Often, the owner of the factory or mine rented out cheap **slum** housing. He might also control the bank. He might even own the shops and taverns. If the owner thought a worker was a troublemaker, he could see to it that no other factory would hire anyone from that worker's family.

An increase in population led to the creation of police forces and the building of more jails. More law enforcement meant that more people were picked up by the police.

Life was hard for the working poor. Overcrowding, bad sanitation, pollution, and poor **nutrition** became more of a problem. So too did disease. When disease struck, rich and poor alike were at risk. The rich moved out of the city. The poor were left behind, to work and endure their new life in the city.

Vocabulary

sanitation, n. the system of keeping a place clean and free of disease

slum, n. a crowded city neighborhood where buildings are in bad condition; often used to refer to areas where poor people live

nutrition, n. the process of eating the right kinds of food to be healthy

During the Industrial Revolution, poor people often lived in cramped housing with bad sanitation.

Chapter 5
The Rise of Capitalism

Great Change in Business "Everywhere, so much change," the newly rich merchant would tell you. Those words would be echoed by the poor, struggling mill hand. Quaint villages had been transformed into bustling, overcrowded cities. Life would never be the same again!

The Big Question

What was mercantilism?

The industrial towns of Great Britain, with their steam-powered factories and growing populations, offered people a different, often harsher, way of life than the rural villages they had left behind.

Machines as large as houses clanked in the once-quiet countryside. The smokestacks of the coal-burning steam engines belched black smoke on every horizon. And so many people were on the move! Everyone was hoping to find a way to make a living. Many dreamed of becoming fabulously rich.

Was there something behind such change? Well, one important factor was the development of **capitalism**. How and why did capitalism grow in importance at this time? How did the Industrial Revolution help capitalist systems develop all around the world? Good questions! Let's first examine what capitalism is.

Vocabulary

capitalism, n. an economic system in which resources and businesses are privately owned and prices are not controlled by the government

capitalist, n. a person who participates in capitalism; a person who sells goods, services, or who invests money in a business

What Is Capitalism?

Capitalism begins with capital. Capital is money invested in the creation of a business, and in its development and growth. Capitalism stimulates the production of cheaper and more efficiently made goods and services. When people, or consumers, buy these goods or services—the **capitalist** hopes to make a profit from his or her investment.

If capitalists think a business activity—whether making a product or offering a service—is not profitable, they will not invest their money. It would be better to invest the capital in starting up some other, more profitable businesses. This determination to make money drives the capitalist to find different kinds of opportunities. It also drives the workers to find jobs so they too can earn money—enough money to live and to purchase the products they and other workers are making. Finally, capitalism tells us that the best use of money is to make more money by investing it in still more business opportunities—and so on and on it goes.

To understand capitalism's power to change the world, we must first understand its roots. Then we can explore the ways it affected how people lived in the 1800s and 1900s. Understanding the history of capitalism will help us appreciate its many strengths—and its weaknesses.

So, when did capitalism begin? As long as people have been around, there have been craftspeople, merchants, and traders who know how to make or buy something cheap and sell it for a profit. In that sense, capitalist activity is as old as civilization itself. But modern high-stakes capitalism is only about 120 years old. But it is possible to trace certain aspects of capitalism to the later Middle Ages, especially in the economic policies of the city-states of northern Italy and in the European nations on the Atlantic Ocean and the North Sea. However, before the rise of capitalism, another economic system of ideas, called **mercantilism**, guided the rulers of these countries.

> **Vocabulary**
> ....
> **mercantilism,** n. an economic system that aims to increase a country's wealth and power by controlling trade and people

Mercantilism

England, France, Spain, and Portugal became rich during the age of exploration. From the 1500s to the early 1700s, shiploads of gold and silver crossed the Atlantic Ocean—plundered from the Americas. Some of these European countries also grew wealthy by enslaving people and forcing them to work in silver and gold mines, or on plantations. Other countries grew wealthy through organized piracy. Still others brought precious goods, such as spices and sugar cane, to European markets and gained great profits. Each country's leaders had to decide how best to use this wealth.

European countries competed to control trade. Trade produced wealth, and wealth brought power.

The mercantilist theory was that a country could grow rich and powerful by controlling trade. If it could force rival nations to buy *its* goods, it could increase the amount of silver and gold *it* had. This was important because the country that had the greatest wealth could dominate all the others.

To achieve such a thing, a country must **export**, or sell, more of its goods than it **imports**, or buys, from other countries. In this way, the profits gained could then be invested into that country. They could be used to build its system of roads and bridges; to deepen its harbors; to develop its mines; to grow more crops—and even to strengthen and expand its military. These investments would make that country stronger and even richer.

Vocabulary

export, v. to send goods to sell in another country

import, v. to bring goods into one country from another country

Many of the kings of Europe were advised that in order to become wealthy and to control trade, they must impose tariffs, or taxes, on goods that were produced by rival countries. That way, those goods would become more expensive and less affordable to people in the home country. And, even if foreign goods were actually sold in the home country, the government would profit from the tariffs or taxes that had been imposed.

The Need for Colonies

To make the mercantile system work, a country needed to establish and control colonies. These colonies provided cheap labor, **raw materials**, and natural resources—especially resources not available in the home country. At the same time, the people in these colonies would become another market for the home country's goods. The people in the colonies would also have to pay taxes for the privilege of living under the protection of the home country. The richer the colony, the richer the home country. This was a powerful argument to conquer and control foreign lands.

> **Vocabulary**
>
> **raw material,** n. something that can be used to make or create a product; for example, cotton is a raw material used to make fabric

Countries that believed in mercantilism passed strict laws that prohibited their colonies from trading with other countries and foreign colonies. Nor could colonial people start up industries of their own, especially if they were in competition with those in the home countries. Britain went so far as to forbid any ships except those flying the British flag from carrying goods to or from its colonies. As for the people in the colonies, they had little say in how the home country taxed them or controlled their developing economy. America revolted against Great Britain in part because it was being taxed *without* being able to have a voice in its own affairs.

European Colonies, 1700–1900

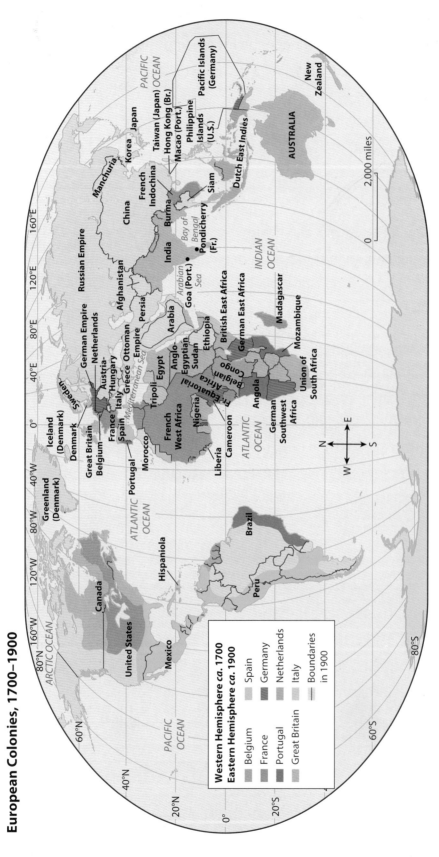

Over a two-hundred-year period, European nations established colonies in most parts of the world.

In the mercantile era, it was also important that agriculture and manufacturing in the home country be highly productive. So governments supported new industries, especially those that produced goods that otherwise would have to be imported. Governments encouraged banks to loan money to new industries. They also created national standards of currency, weights, and measures, which made **commerce** easier. And, as always, new business ideas were emerging. These new ideas were linked to industry, a new age, and new ways to make money.

Vocabulary

commerce, n. the buying and selling of goods and services; trade

Chapter 6
Adam Smith

New Economic Ideas Gradually, a new kind of capitalism emerged—industrial capitalism. Industrial capitalism differed from mercantilism. Industrial capitalists made their money by investing in factories, *not* in trade. And, as industrial capitalists grew wealthy, they wanted to gain political power to match their growing wealth. They found their spokesperson in Scottish-born Adam Smith.

The Big Question

What were Adam Smith's basic economic beliefs?

Adam Smith was both a student of capitalism and a supporter of it. He gave people ideas and terms that would help them understand the changes that were transforming their lives, and he is remembered today as capitalism's first great champion.

This statue of Adam Smith stands outside St. Giles' Cathedral in Edinburgh, Scotland.

Adam Smith and Modern Capitalism

Adam Smith was born in 1723, in Scotland. By the time he was born, Scotland was part of Great Britain and was prospering economically. Adam Smith's parents saw to it that their son had a good education. He studied at the university in Glasgow, famous for its fine, enlightened teachers. With a scholarship, he also studied at Oxford in England. But Smith preferred his native Scotland. Soon, he was teaching at the university in Glasgow.

Smith was particularly interested in the way society offered each person a measure of justice or freedom. For him, this was not just a matter of **civil rights** and living under the protection of fair courts. It was also a matter of how people earned a living, acquired the things they needed, and exchanged necessary services with each other. Smith was asking economic questions—questions about money and resources. In 1776, Adam Smith published *The Wealth of Nations*. His book is one of the most important studies of **economics** that has ever been written.

Vocabulary

civil rights, n. the rights that all citizens are supposed to have

economics, n. the study of the management of money and resources to produce, buy, and sell goods and services

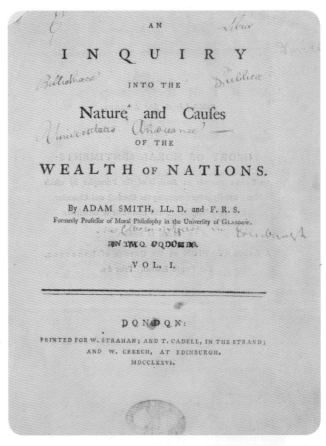

The Wealth of Nations is still an important text in the study of economics.

Supply and Demand

Smith described what he saw as a wonderful balance in economic relations. In every setting in which two willing and freely acting people wanted to exchange goods or services for money, he found a law at work: the law of **supply and demand**. When a seller set a price for goods or services, a buyer would either pay it or not. If the seller thought he could sell what he had to offer to someone else, he was not worried. But if he felt he might not find another buyer, he might drop the price.

Likewise, a buyer would have to consider whether he could get what he wanted somewhere else for less. If not, and if he really wanted what the seller had to offer, he would have to pay what the seller wanted. Smith said this law was at work every time a good or a service was bought or sold. It was, he said, as though an "Invisible Hand" adjusted each and every transaction. Even if it only took place in the minds of the buyer and the seller, the law of supply and demand eventually determined the worth of whatever was being exchanged. As buyers and sellers tried to get the best deal for themselves, they would establish what something was worth and be satisfied that they got a fair deal.

It was important, Smith said, that no one interfere with this fair, natural balance between supply and demand. Smith was against anything that gave anyone an unfair advantage in the marketplace. He felt that the government should step in to prevent unfair advantages. In general, however, Smith believed it was best for the government to do nothing more than it absolutely had to do to maintain fairness in manufacturing and trade. This hands-off policy is known as *laissez-faire* (/less*ay/fayr/), a French phrase that means "to let happen." In economics, it refers to the idea that government should allow the marketplace to act or work all by itself.

> ## Vocabulary
>
> **supply and demand,** n. the amount of goods and services available to buy compared with the amount that people want to buy
>
> **laissez-faire,** n. a philosophy that calls for very little or no government involvement in the economy

Division of Labor

Adam Smith also wrote about the **division of labor**. Imagine, Smith said, that one person alone was trying to make pins to sell. He would have his hands full. Making a single pin would be quite complicated: smelting the metal, drawing the wire, cutting it, and sharpening it, then packaging a bunch of pins, taking them to market, dealing with customers, and so on. It would be a dreadfully slow and costly process. There had to be a better, more efficient way.

Vocabulary

division of labor, n. the breakdown of work into specific tasks performed by different people; often considered a way to make workers more efficient

What if several people all worked together under one roof in a pin factory? Each person would specialize in a different step in the process. Each person would be an expert for one part of the process of making pins. This would be a division of labor.

Smith saw how workers in a pin factory could produce many more pins much faster than a single pin-maker could all alone in a little shop. Factory pins would cost much less. They might even be better pins. The consumer would benefit. And so would the capitalist who owned the factory. In fact, he probably would make a handsome profit.

What should the capitalist do with this profit? Smith argued that the profit should be used to make more profit. A pin-factory owner, for example, might use his profit to build up a supply of metal, or buy some new tools to improve production. Or maybe he would expand his business and begin to produce needles. Or maybe invest in a coal mine or steam engines—anything that seemed to be a good way to gain even more profit. It seemed that the sky was the limit!

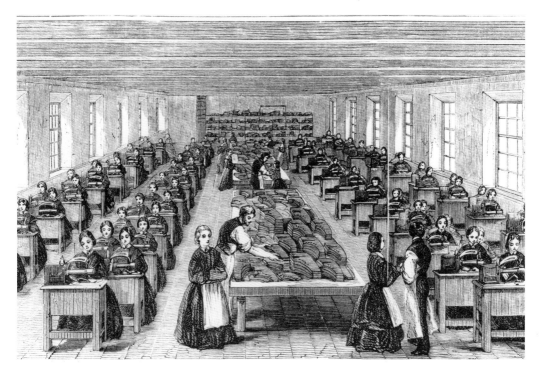

Workers in this shoe factory concentrated on separate, specific tasks.

Smith marveled at how a healthy and fair economy not only adjusts or manages itself but also provides for its own growth and improvement. By stressing the importance of a free market and showing how greater efficiency of production would produce a higher standard of living, Adam Smith became a great supporter of widespread industrialization and the spread of capitalism. Thanks in part to him, our world has never been the same since.

Chapter 7
Living in the Industrial Era

Growing Gap Between Rich and Poor

As the Industrial Revolution spread, many people became very rich. Many more, however, stayed quite poor and lived in misery. The gap between rich and poor grew at an alarming rate.

The Big Question

What were the advantages and disadvantages of the industrial era?

Stories about hard-hearted factory owners and struggling workers trying to earn a living tell us just how hard these times were. No one described living and working conditions more powerfully than the British writer Charles Dickens.

Charles Dickens

Dickens knew firsthand what it meant to be poor. Born in Portsmouth, England, in 1812, Dickens lived comfortably enough until he was twelve. However, his father's bad management of the family's finances led to disaster. Because his father couldn't pay the family's bills, Charles had to quit school and go to work in a factory. His father, mother, and younger brothers and sisters were all sent to **debtors' prison** until the family could pay their bills.

Vocabulary

"debtors' prison," (phrase) a jail for people who could not pay money that they owed

Charles Dickens experienced firsthand what it meant to be poor. As a twelve-year-old, he had to go to work in a factory.

Young Charles wasn't used to the rough, hard life of London's streets. He was stunned by what he saw every day and night. He spent the rest of his life writing novels about the hardships of being poor, especially of being a poor child.

Dickens was a marvelous author. His stories are sometimes funny and sometimes sad. Although they may exaggerate, or stretch, what he saw around him, they are always sensitive and sympathetic to the suffering Dickens witnessed as a boy.

One of Dickens's most vivid novels is *Hard Times*. It tells the story of rich and poor people living in "Coketown," a sooty, cramped industrial English city where poor workers and their children were mistrusted and abused. It is based on an actual English city of the 1850s.

Another of Dickens's novels, *Oliver Twist*, tells the story of a young orphan forced to live in London's streets among criminals and gangs. Although Dickens made up the characters, they, too, were based on real life.

You may know Dickens's most famous story, *A Christmas Carol*. It has a happy ending: poor little Tiny Tim and his family have a merry Christmas after all, once stingy old Scrooge learns how important it is to share his wealth. Dickens hoped his readers would learn this lesson—and not just at Christmastime.

In the novel *Oliver Twist*, Oliver finds himself in the poorhouse. One of the most famous scenes in the book is when Oliver, who is feeling very hungry, asks for more food. This scene is shown here.

Even people who didn't read Charles Dickens's stories could see them performed as plays on the stage. Thanks in part to the writings of Dickens, social reformers began working to improve living and working conditions for the poor.

Benjamin Disraeli

One such reformer went on to become one of the most important political leaders of the 1800s. Benjamin Disraeli (/dihz*ray*lee/) was twice elected **prime minister** of Great Britain. As the leader of the Conservative Party and Queen Victoria's favorite politician, Disraeli helped pass many laws that benefited the working classes.

> **Vocabulary**
>
> **prime minister,** n. the head of government in some countries

As a young man, Disraeli wrote novels. Although not as popular a writer as Dickens, Disraeli also brought attention to the poor in the Industrial Revolution. His novel, *Sybil, or The Two Nations*, written in 1842, describes the gap between the rich and poor. It was, he wrote, as though there were:

> Two nations: between whom there is no [communication] and no sympathy; who are as ignorant of each other's habits, thoughts, and feelings, as if they were dwellers in different zones or inhabitants of different planets; who are formed by a different breeding, are fed by a different food, are ordered by different manners, and are not governed by the same laws.

Disraeli worried about how the rich and poor would get along in such a divided nation. He and many others at the time worried about violent conflicts between rich and poor. Day-to-day stress was as much a product of the Industrial Revolution as iron, cloth, and bustling business.

Benjamin Disraeli (right) was a favorite of Britain's Queen Victoria (seated).

The Upper Class

Historians learn a great deal about an era by studying how people furnished their homes, what they ate, where and how they traveled, when and where they organized social events, and what games they played. Of course, these things varied depending on a person's wealth and social standing—or class.

If you belonged to the landowning aristocracy, you would probably have a lot of servants to cook and clean for you, and to take care of your household's needs. You would also probably hire someone to manage your finances. You would therefore have a lot of leisure time, which you might spend hunting on horseback, visiting neighbors, going to balls, or traveling abroad.

Members of the upper class had much more time for leisure activities than most other people at this time in history.

If you were a successful capitalist, you would probably work very hard managing your affairs and would try to invest most of your profits to bring in even more money. But there would probably be enough left over to live comfortably and maybe go into **politics**. Your money might not buy happiness, but it could certainly buy you a life of luxury.

Vocabulary

politics, n. the activities of leaders running a government

The Middle Class

If you were a member of the middle class—say, a shopkeeper—you had to work regular hours. Even though you might have some servants, too, you couldn't do whatever you wanted to do as often as a rich person might.

If you were a good, hardworking, and skillful lawyer or doctor with wealthy patients, you might earn a comfortable living. If you had a shop or were a skilled craftsperson, say, a clockmaker or a fine tailor, you had to serve your customers' needs. You would be working with your hands but not under the same pressures or hardships as some factory workers. You would probably be your own boss.

In your leisure time, you might be able to pursue a hobby or read. Unlike poorer folk, you could afford the candles and the coal that would keep your rooms lit and warm in the evenings.

When you could, you might travel by train to the coast or take long walks in the country. Perhaps you would take an interest in the history of your town. You might even become an amateur astronomer with a small telescope you made yourself. You certainly would meet regularly with your friends in a social club or at a local tavern or inn.

The Working Poor

Only about 20 percent of all the people in the 1800s were upper class or middle class. What about the other 80 percent? How did they spend their leisure time? Did they even have leisure time?

Certainly, the poor did not have much leisure time. The poorer you were, the more you worried about putting food on the table and a roof over your head. You had precious little time for amusements or distractions. And if you were out of work with nothing to do, how could you afford anything, even the barest necessities? Even if the state required children between the ages of seven and fourteen to go to school, parents often were against it. They tried to avoid any law that prevented their children from working. Poor families needed whatever children could add to their pitiful income.

Despite the hardships suffered by the working poor, they did on occasion find time to enjoy life. Music, card games, the circus, the zoo, fairs, and public parks offered forms of relaxation and entertainment. Team sports—especially soccer and rugby—became very popular in Britain. In America during this time, baseball drew large crowds.

There was a great contrast between the lives of the rich and the poor in Britain in the 1800s.

Churches and other places of worship offered a source of comfort and companionship. Many people took comfort from their faith when life was particularly difficult. A place of worship was often the focal point, or center, for small communities.

Crime, Punishment, and Migration

Modern police forces as we know them date from this period. They were created, in part, as a response to having such large populations of people living in cities. With an increased population, and a larger police force, crimes like begging, stealing, and drunkenness were more commonly reported.

Sometimes poor workers packed up and went in search of a better life. A worker might hear from a friend or a family member about work and better conditions in another city or town. The biggest gamble was leaving for another country, especially one far away from home and family. The trip cost years of savings. There was no certainty of finding work, just a vague promise in an advertisement or a rumor. And yet millions of people migrated to foreign lands, especially to North America, during the Industrial Revolution. Some of them might even have been your ancestors.

For some people, the world was changing a little too fast for their liking. Most tried to find their place in the developing industrial world. But there were those who fought against the age of the machine.

For some people, the Industrial Revolution was a marvelous age. The wonders of the Industrial Revolution were displayed in 1851, in the Crystal Palace, a British exhibition hall in London, England, that looked like a giant greenhouse. It was built with cast-iron supports and nearly three hundred thousand panes of glass.

Chapter 8
Protesting Industrialization

"Long live King Ludd! Long live our king!" Just around midnight, twelve masked men broke down a door and ran shouting into a dark factory. Swinging lead pipes and hammers, they attacked the weaving machines with such fury you might have thought the machines were evil monsters.

The Big Question

Why did workers begin to organize themselves into groups?

Vocabulary

Luddite, n. in the early 1800s, a person who protested against industrialization by destroying machines and factories; today, the word refers to someone who is opposed to new ideas or technologies

That's exactly what the men thought. For good measure, after they finished, the men set the building on fire. It was 1812. The **Luddites** had struck again.

Why did these desperate Englishmen think that weaving machines were their enemies? What had happened to them? Who was King Ludd, anyway? The answers to these questions have to do with a protest movement against industrialization.

Not everyone thought that the coming of the Industrial Age was a good thing. The Luddites destroyed machines and factories to show their anger at the miseries caused by the Industrial Revolution.

Stopping "Progress"

Like most great changes in history, the Industrial
Revolution created winners and losers. The winners
were the industrialists who founded successful
factories and, to a lesser extent, the consumers who
were able to buy cheaper goods. The losers included
unskilled workers, many of whom had to endure
exhausting and dangerous working conditions, and

Vocabulary

industrialism, n.
the organization of
society around an
economy based on
the use of machines
and factories

skilled workers, many of whom were replaced by machines. The winners hailed
industrialism as "progress," but many of the losers condemned it as unfair, and
even wicked. If this was "progress," they were opposed to it.

Some of those on the losing side of progress believed that something
extreme had to be done to stop industrialism. They believed that the
machines had put them out of work and made their lives miserable, and they
hated the machines with a passion. Their anger went back to the earliest days
of the Industrial Revolution.

Women and children provided cheap labor and enabled factory owners to make greater profits.

62

Although many families who farmed the land had wanted to stay in their ancestral villages, it made more sense for the poorer ones to go to larger towns and cities where they might find work. Those who found work in factories and mines were often women and children. This work did not require much skill. The pay was small, but it was something.

Often, skilled workers were not wanted—or needed. Men in particular had great trouble adjusting to the new conditions. Their pride was wounded when their wives and daughters found work while they stayed idle. In their minds, the new machines made them less important.

The Luddites

Some discontented workers formed secret societies and tried to stop the Industrial Revolution. One group was called the Luddites. They were active in the weaving districts of Britain between 1811 and 1816.

The Luddites claimed they were following "Ned Ludd," but historians have no record of him. Ludd was probably a mythical figure. Or maybe the name was an alias for the Luddites' real leader.

Adopting the mythical figure of Ludd as their king, the men sent demanding messages to the owners of textile factories. Some demanded that the new weaving machines be removed, or, if not removed, reduced in number. When the owners refused, some Luddites attacked.

Elsewhere in Europe over the next several decades, the authorities crushed similar movements among weavers and other craftspeople. In hard times, however, uprisings among workers would appear again.

Workingmen's Associations

While factories and mines brought many workers together in the new industrial cities, some workers saw an advantage in organizing themselves into groups. This was their best hope, they felt, if they were going to maintain their dignity. Modern unions trace their beginnings to these efforts.

At first, workingmen's associations used membership **dues** (often only a penny or two per month) to help cover the funeral costs of a member who had died on the job. They also helped struggling widows and orphans. Sometimes the associations would support community projects or organize a summer picnic. They might sponsor a sports team or a marching band.

Vocabulary

dues, n. money paid to an organization to become a member of that organization

Strikes

Gradually, these associations began voicing concerns about their working conditions and pay to their employers and even to the government. They reasoned that they would be stronger if they stuck together to voice their common complaints and demands. It was a risky business. The owners fired many workers who were thought to be organizers or troublemakers. Often, a worker's name was passed around to other owners, and the person would never be hired again.

Quite often, going on strike did not achieve the desired outcome. And sometimes, strikers lost their jobs.

Workers often demanded higher wages or better working conditions. Most often the owners refused. Then the workers either had to accept the owners' decisions or go on **strike**.

Vocabulary

strike, n. a temporary work stoppage organized by workers as a protest

The owners usually would bring in other workers—strikebreakers—to keep their factories going. Or they might close down the factories until the workers begged to go back to work for the same low wages.

If things got out of hand from the owners' point of view, company-paid security people, the police, even the army, were usually not far away. During this period and well into the 1900s in many industrializing countries, strikes were illegal. Striking workers often encountered violent conflicts with nonstrikers and the authorities. Many striking workers were arrested and treated harshly in the courts.

However, it would not be true to say that workers were always completely unsuccessful when demanding better wages or working conditions. Often they achieved minor successes, which ultimately led to further changes or improvements at a later date. For example, American women working in a textile mill in Lowell, Massachusetts, went on strike in 1834 when their wages were cut, even though they were expected to work for thirteen hours each day. They were unsuccessful in overturning the mill owner's decision, but over time, they went on to organize women in other textile mills, which meant that working women were joining together around a common issue. The Lowell Women formed a Labor Reform Association and demonstrated that being organized and united was the best way to work for necessary changes. They sent signed petitions to people in power, and this ultimately led to investigations and public hearings about working conditions. Not until 1853 was the length of the working day in America reduced—but it would not have happened without that important first step by a group of women.

Chapter 9
Robert Owen

Changes Some factory owners were fair and kind toward their workers. One of the fairest and kindest was Robert Owen, perhaps because he worked for a kind cloth seller as a boy. Owen was born in Newtown, Wales, in 1771. Although he only went to school until he was ten, he loved to read. Often, young Robert was found in his employer's private library.

The Big Question

What did Robert Owen do to achieve better living and working conditions for people?

By the age of nineteen, Robert Owen was superintendent of a large cotton mill in Manchester. The mill prospered when he used a fine grade of American cotton and introduced other improvements. Soon, he became a manager and then a partner in the mill.

Owen urged his partners to buy another mill in New Lanark, Scotland. The town displayed the worst of the new industrial world: pollution, crime, bad housing, and despair among the people.

Robert Owen was both an industrialist and a reformer. He believed that it was the duty of factory owners to improve working conditions for people.

Improved Conditions

Owen changed all that by investing in better living and working conditions. In 1816, the first day-care center for small children opened. Workers could buy certain things at very low prices. He managed the sale of alcohol. The workers' spirits improved, and the mill prospered. Thanks to Owen, New Lanark became a happier place to live and work.

Robert Owen began to write about his experiences and ideas for reform. In 1813, he published *A New View of Society, or Essays on the Principle of the Formulation of the Human Character.* In this and other writings, he argued for improved schooling. Just as important, he argued that machines should not dominate men.

Instead, Owens argued, through kindness and respect for workers, society could find harmony and peace. Owen devised elaborate plans for a perfect community, including many of the reforms he introduced at New Lanark. He envisioned such working and living communities all over the world.

This is an artist's impression of New Lanark. Of course, it did not look exactly like this— but the living and working conditions were much better than in other industrial towns of the time.

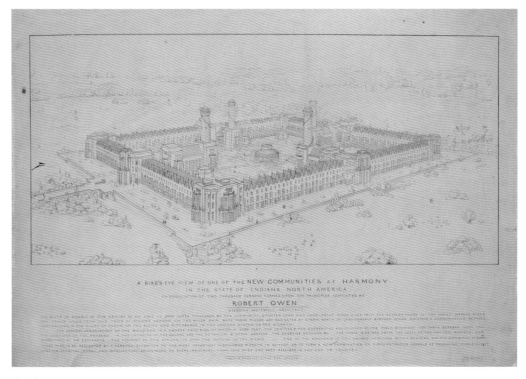

A BIRD'S EYE VIEW OF ONE OF THE NEW COMMUNITIES AT HARMONY.
IN THE STATE OF INDIANA NORTH AMERICA
IN ASSOCIATION OF TWO THOUSAND PERSONS FORMED UPON THE PRINCIPLES ADVOCATED BY
ROBERT OWEN

Owen's ideas for improving the lives of working people traveled across the ocean to America. This plan is of a community called New Harmony in Indiana.

Some of these communities actually started up in America. Owen bought thirty thousand acres in Indiana and founded the town of New Harmony. But internal disagreements caused it to fail after three years. When Owen returned to Britain, he had lost 80 percent of his wealth.

Still, Owen's ideas won many followers, especially among younger workers. They took his ideas into the union movement. Robert Owen, still enthusiastic for reform, died at age eighty-two in the same town in Wales where he was born. He probably did not realize how important his leadership had been at a crucial time in the Industrial Revolution.

Socialism

Robert Owen was an early believer in **socialism**. Generally, socialists believe in a system where there is government ownership of the production,

Vocabulary

socialism, n. an economic system in which major industries are owned or regulated by the government, rather than by private businesses

69

distribution, and sale of products or goods. In other words, the government owns and **regulates** certain industries or businesses for the benefit of the community as a whole—or the public good.

Socialists want to prevent problems that they believe come from unchecked capitalism, such as poor treatment of workers and the gap between rich and poor. There are varying views among socialists as to how exactly this should be done. Many would probably argue that capitalism in its purest form can cause great harm.

Owen's hope was that capitalism could be reformed peacefully and through common agreement. Wealthy employers, he thought, would voluntarily share their wealth with the workers, just as he did. His kind of socialist thinking is often called **utopian**. A utopia is an imagined, perfect place that doesn't exist in this world. To call Owen's ideas utopian socialism implies that they are impractical.

Other socialists argued that the rich would only share their wealth with the poor when they were forced to do so. In the next chapter you will learn about Karl Marx. More than anyone else, Marx thought there would have to be a violent revolution if real change was going to happen.

It's important to understand that there is indeed a third social and political system that is neither completely socialist nor completely capitalist. Today across much of Europe, capitalism and socialism have been combined, or interwoven, to form what is called a **social democracy**. Quite simply, these nations have incorporated both capitalist and socialist principles into their structures of government and into their societies as a whole.

> ## Vocabulary
>
> **regulate,** v. to control or place limits on
>
> **utopian,** adj. idealistic; usually describes beliefs about the perfect society
>
> **social democracy,** n. a system of representative government that uses elements of capitalism and socialism to govern the economy

New View of Society.

TRACTS

RELATIVE TO THIS SUBJECT;

VIZ.

Proposals for Raising a Colledge of Industry of all useful Trades and Husbandry. By JOHN BELLERS.

(Reprinted from the Original, published in the year 1696).

Report to the Committee of the Association for the Relief of the Manufacturing and Labouring Poor.

A Brief Sketch of the religious Society of People called Shakers.

WITH

AN ACCOUNT OF THE PUBLIC PROCEEDINGS

CONNECTED WITH THE SUBJECT,

Which took place in London in July and August 1817.

PUBLISHED

By ROBERT OWEN.

London:

PRINTED FOR LONGMAN, HURST, REES, ORME, AND BROWN, PATER-
NOSTER ROW; CADELL AND DAVIES, STRAND; J. HATCHARD, PICCA-
DILLY; MURRAY, ALBEMARLE-STREET; CONSTABLE AND CO., AND
OLIPHANT AND CO., EDINBURGH; SMITH AND SONS, AND BRASH
AND REID, GLASGOW; AND SOLD BY ALL THE BOOKSELLERS IN
TOWN AND COUNTRY.

1818.

Here you can see the title page of Robert Owen's *A New View of Society*.

Chapter 10
Looking for a New Economic Order

Good Times and Bad During good times in the industrial era, most people are able to find work. They usually earn enough money to afford their basic needs and maybe even a bit extra for something special. But in bad times, with a lot of people out of work, wages tend to fall. Then, workers cannot afford to buy as many of the things they need. This causes manufacturers to cut back on production and lay off still more workers. Soon, the whole economy begins to slow down. This is called a depression.

The Big Question

What factors within the capitalist system caused a degree of unpredictability in relation to the well-being of the workers?

Laissez-faire economists, you remember, thought the capitalist system should be allowed to find its natural balance through the law of supply and demand in the marketplace. Even if times were bad, they thought nothing should be done to affect the price of goods and services. Eventually, things would get better. How?

Typically, when the economy is strong and there are lots of jobs, people tend to spend more money.

In the midst of economic and social misery, some daring **investors** will see a way to make a profit. These investors risk their capital in new businesses and manufacturing enterprises. This begins to put people back to work. As workers see better times ahead and begin to spend their wages, they stimulate, or boost, the economy. Soon other capitalists see ways to make profits. Eventually, good times return and most people are working again.

In good times, however, wages rise—but so too can the prices of all kinds of goods and necessities. This is because of a number of factors, including the law of supply and demand. A rise in prices can set in motion something called **inflation**. Inflation happens when the money supply in a nation is increased, which in turn decreases, or devalues, a nation's currency—for example the dollar. So, as a dollar becomes worth less, prices go up to maintain levels of profit for the manufacturers.

> ## Vocabulary
>
> **investor,** n. a person who puts money into a business with the goal of later making a profit
>
> **inflation,** n. a rise in prices and a fall in the purchasing value of money

And so people have to spend more money to purchase things. Eventually, it becomes more difficult for capitalists to make a profit and compete in the marketplace. Their businesses fail. They lay off workers. Then, prices fall. The economy starts to swing back down again. Now, we're back again where we started. Up and down. Good times and bad. These *business cycles*—periods of high employment and prosperity alternating with periods of low employment and general economic distress—seemed to be as sure as the seasons. It is hard to predict when the first snow will fall in winter or when the first blade of grass will begin to grow in spring, but you still know that winter and spring are going to happen. Most economists made a similar argument about business cycles. They could not say for sure when the cycles would begin and end, but they felt sure that these cycles would continue.

Philosophers, economists, social reformers, religious leaders, and many politicians worried about these business cycles, about the poor, about the discontent of workers, about crime and pollution. Was there any way, they wondered, to establish social harmony? Could we ever overcome the feeling of being controlled by **impersonal** forces? Can a modern economy avoid these business cycles?

┌──────────────────────────────┐
Vocabulary
···
impersonal, adj. having no connection to people; lacking feeling
└──────────────────────────────┘

Hoping for a Revolution

In the 1840s, bad times seemed to be increasing all across Europe. Desperate factory workers threatened strikes in Europe's most industrialized cities. In the countryside, farmers complained of absurdly low prices for their produce. To stop public protests, governments called out the police and the army. Could anything prevent these confrontations?

Would factory owners voluntarily give their workers better wages and improve working conditions, as Robert Owen and a few other idealists hoped? Most observers thought this approach was unrealistic.

A revolutionary uprising began in France in 1848 and spread across Europe. People demanded more involvement in government, freedom of the press, and better working conditions. But these uprisings were not very well organized. This image shows an uprising in Germany in 1848.

Perhaps the governments would give in and agree to some of the workers' demands for fair wages, better working conditions, and broader democracy. Not likely, given the prevailing belief in laissez-faire economics. Regulating business, most politicians thought, would be harmful to their own best interests.

Many people assumed that there were only two possible outcomes. Either the governments would crush the workers and teach them to meekly accept their hard fate, or the workers would revolt, overthrow the governments, and radically change the capitalist system.

By 1848, things seemed to reach a critical point. Revolutions broke out all over Europe. Among the people who called for change that revolutionary year, none had looked forward to a workers' revolution more passionately than Karl Marx, one of Western civilization's most important thinkers.

The Communist Manifesto

In 1848, Marx and his lifelong friend and supporter, Friedrich Engels, published a powerful pamphlet, The **Communist** Manifesto. It called for a workers' revolution to overthrow capitalism. But Marx and Engels didn't just call for this revolution, they predicted that the revolution would occur very soon. When it did, the workers (whom Marx and Engels called **proletarians**) would set up a dictatorship of workers—a dictatorship of the proletariat—that would abolish private ownership, of businesses and of property. A new communist society would emerge. The people would own everything— property and businesses—together. Government would disappear. With no private ownership, there would be no rich or poor. Everyone would be equal. Everyone would work for the common good. There would be no police, laws, courts, or army. Communism would be the purest form of democracy because it would be based on pure equality. The people would govern themselves.

> **Vocabulary**
>
> **communist,** adj. relating to communism, an economic system based on community ownership of property and industry
>
> **proletarian,** n. a worker

Of course, said Marx and Engels, capitalists would never voluntarily give up their profits. Therefore, the workers must rise up in revolution. The pamphlet concludes with a famous rallying cry:

> The proletarians have nothing to lose but their chains. They have a world to win. Workingmen of all countries, unite!

Karl Marx

Stopping the Revolution

Marx and Engels were too optimistic. All across Europe the strikes and revolutionary movements that peaked in 1848 fizzled out. Police and armed forces killed hundreds of workers. Thousands more were arrested and sent to jail. Many emigrated to the United States.

Marx himself fled certain arrest in his native Germany. He settled in London. Engels later joined him. The two men worked hard to organize an international movement of communist revolutionaries. But the revolution that Marx prophesied never happened. Disappointed, but still confident that someday

Friedrich Engels

he would be proven correct, Marx studied and wrote about capitalism. His life's work, *Capital* or *Das Kapital*, a study of capitalism, earned him a reputation as a powerful economic thinker. When he died in 1883 in London, however, only eleven people attended his funeral. Communist revolutions in some countries in the 1900s claimed Marx as a guiding light, but the societies they created were very different from what Marx had envisioned. You will read more about the reasons for this in the next chapter.

Chapter 11
Karl Marx

Revolutionary Karl Marx was born in 1818. By the time he was in his twenties, the Industrial Revolution was bringing his native Germany many of the same conditions it had brought to Great Britain. Marx was distressed by these changes, especially the growing gap between the rich and the poor.

The Big Question

What were the basic differences between the beliefs of Robert Owen and those of Karl Marx?

Marx hoped for a time when everyone on Earth would be equal. This equality would not just be based on fundamental human rights. What good was equality before the law, he thought, if you were starving or didn't have a roof over your head? He wanted to see a day when no one would have any greater economic advantage than anyone else did. Only then, Marx felt, would everyone be truly equal.

Money and the ability to make money, he said, were the most important things. Everything else—the way people were governed, the conditions under which most people lived and worked, education, health care, and other social concerns—was determined by the people who had money.

Marx wanted to know what made human society so stormy and violent. He decided it was because, throughout history, wealth and property were always distributed unevenly. Wherever he looked into the past, he saw a constant conflict between those who had property—he called them the *haves*—and those who had no property, the *have-nots*.

Karl Marx believed that the most powerful and influential people in society were those with the most money.

Class Struggle

Marx called this conflict the *class struggle*. Marx saw that the haves never hesitated to use force to keep what they had. And the have-nots understandably used force to try and capture the haves' possessions. Those who held property controlled the means to produce wealth. Those who did not were at a great disadvantage.

Each historical period, Marx believed, experienced the class struggle between the haves and the have-nots. Out of the powerful struggle would come a new economic system that would overthrow the old one and replace it with a more efficient one.

Marx thought that having or not having material wealth was the most important force in history. He thought he had discovered a law about human affairs as valid as any scientific law for the physical universe. He envied Charles Darwin and Isaac Newton for their certainty about the laws that governed the natural world. He wanted to do the same for human behavior.

The Coming Revolution

In the industrial era, the class struggle had, according to Marx, reached a critical phase. The wealthy upper and middle classes were now combined into what Marx called the **bourgeoisie** (/boor*jwah*zee/). They were the haves, using capitalism to become richer and more powerful. According to Marx, they controlled everything.

> **Vocabulary**
>
> **bourgeoisie,** n. the upper or wealthy middle class; the people who owned the means of production, or what Karl Marx called "the haves"

Though not all of the bourgeoisie were rich, they all enjoyed much greater privileges than did the much poorer have-nots. The have-nots, or workers, whom Marx labeled the proletarians, were forced to accept low wages and harsh working conditions in order to earn enough to survive. They controlled nothing, because they had nothing.

Karl Marx believed that the working class would have to join together if changes were to happen.

If the proletarians could join together against the workers' common enemy, the bourgeoisie, they would have enormous strength. But the bourgeoisie had laws, courts, jails, and armies to prevent that from happening. Just as important, they controlled the schools and the newspapers. Even many religious leaders taught duty, self-sacrifice, and respect for the ruling classes. All of this combined, said Marx, to spread the **propaganda** that kept the bourgeoisie in power.

Vocabulary

propaganda, n. false or exaggerated information that is spread to encourage belief in a certain person or idea

Marx and Capitalism

Marx appreciated many of the improvements brought about by the Industrial Revolution. Machines, he knew, saved time. And they didn't complain. But machines dominated the workers. Marx and other socialists thought it should be the other way around.

Marx also saw that capitalism was an efficient way to invest in and create greater economic productivity. When more things were produced, more people would benefit. This matched his belief that humankind was moving toward a time when there would be better living conditions for everyone. This was in keeping with the ideas of the Enlightenment. But how would this progress come about?

After studying German philosophy and English economic theories and practices, Marx thought he had found an answer. He believed that capitalism naturally contained the seeds of its own destruction. In the process of penetrating every aspect of modern society, capitalism eventually would result in a horribly unequal distribution of wealth. This would make the class struggle even more bitter.

Eventually, Marx believed, the workers would band together and rise up against the capitalists who held them in economic slavery. They would **confiscate**

Vocabulary

confiscate, v. to take away; to seize

Karl Marx thought revolution was inevitable.

all private property and place it in the hands of a revolutionary government that would protect the workers' interests. The have-nots would triumph through the sheer force of their numbers. Robert Owen, you will recall, thought socialism could be achieved voluntarily. Marx thought it would be achieved only through a violent revolution.

A New Economic Order

Marx predicted that the revolution would go through two stages. First, the proletariat would successfully revolt against the bourgeoisie. In this phase, the proletariat would establish a socialist government, representing all workers. He called this government a dictatorship of the proletariat. This government would own all the factories and regulate their production. No one would be able to accumulate wealth and power.

This socialist government would decide what should be produced and how much it should cost; what wages should be paid; and what benefits each citizen was entitled to. Everyone would be paid a fair wage. No one would be forced to work in unsafe conditions or for long hours.

Just as important, the state would control all services: transportation, housing, medical care, education, the media, and entertainment. All these would be free or very inexpensive. In theory, no one would have any greater privileges than anyone else had. Everyone would become perfectly equal.

This would set the stage for the second stage of the revolution: the establishment of what Marx called communism. After a time (Marx was never clear about exactly when or how this would happen), the socialist state itself—the government—would just wither away. People would own and control everything together, as a community. Hence, the name *communism*.

Marx imagined that when everyone was equal, each person would have whatever was essential for a happy life. What would emerge would be a "classless society," with no conflict or violence. No one would envy anyone else. There would be no need for the police or courts or jails or even laws. When this point was reached, there would be no need for government itself. There would be no government anywhere in the world!

With worldwide equality among peoples, there would be no need for national pride or ambitions. With no rivalries among nations, there would be no need for war! You can see how Marx's ideas would attract many people—especially the poor and those who felt the pain of economic depression.

Marx seemed to believe that the people in control of the socialist state, the dictatorship of the proletariat, would not use their power to gain benefits for themselves and their followers. Nor did he imagine that they would ever act unfairly toward anyone who opposed them. He sincerely believed they would willingly give up their power to achieve the communist ideal.

Marx seems to have underestimated the degree to which ambition, desire, and a thirst for competition drive human beings to raise themselves above others. Although they have caused serious problems in history, these urges have also inspired marvelous creativity. These urges are at the heart of our civilization.

Marx's Legacy

Karl Marx got many people thinking about socialism. His promise of a better future for the working classes inspired millions. His thinking has also motivated countless people to criticize him. As they have done so, they have clarified their own thinking about past, present, and future relationships between economics and politics.

Since the 1900s, a few nations have called themselves communist, or "people's democracies." Most of these countries, however, have been led by dictators and have brought neither equality nor democracy. They are more accurately called

> **Vocabulary**
> ....
> **totalitarian,** adj.
> controlling all
> aspects of life

totalitarian socialist nations, because the government controls not only production but every aspect of society. People in control of these states tend to use their power to benefit themselves and their followers. Workers generally have less freedom in these systems than they would under capitalism. In many ways, these countries are the opposite of Marx's communist ideal.

Many people believe that a communist revolution is not necessary. Instead, they place their hope in democratic reforms, protection of civil liberties, and laws that require capitalists to abide by strict rules. These measures, they argue, will protect the worker, the consumer, and the environment from the excesses of capitalism.

Although many people disagree with Karl Marx, others continue to find value in his ideas. His works give us a greater understanding of the times he lived in and remain important today.

Chapter 12
In Our Time

Patience in Our Time If Patience Kershaw could travel into the present, what would she think? We can make some good guesses to answer this question, based on what we have learned.

"Your cities are enormous!" she might exclaim. "The buildings are so tall, and so many seem to be made of glass! But where do you keep all the horses?"

The Big Question

How would you describe the changes taking place in the Information Age in comparison to the first and second stages of the Industrial Revolution?

You might smile and tell her that cars and trucks have replaced horses. We still have trains, you'd say, but they are much bigger and faster than any from her time.

As early morning traffic whizzes by, Patience might not know what to look at first. "Where are all these people going?" she might ask.

And you might reply, "Most are going to work. Those big yellow buses are taking children to school. The trucks may be taking things from factories to stores, or even to other countries."

Vocabulary

atomic energy, n. energy that is created by splitting an atom; also called nuclear energy

When Patience sees her first airplane, she might collapse with fright. You might tell her that planes, just like cars, trucks, trains, and even ships, run on fuel made from petroleum—oil. Of course, you have to tell her what that is, too. You will probably avoid the subject of **atomic energy**!

Chicago is a modern city that could not even have been imagined at the beginning of the Industrial Revolution.

Would Patience understand radios and televisions? Or telephones? Or computers? She might ask, "How do these words and pictures fly through the air?"

Patience would ask about your clothing, especially the items made from man-made fibers. And she would ask about modern materials, such as plastic and steel. Almost everything would either intrigue or bewilder her.

Finally, Patience might say, "Stop! Where did all of these things come from? How did all of these changes happen?"

The Ongoing Revolution

Having read this book, you might be able to give Patience some answers. But you might also want to ask a historian to help you explain. A historian would tell you that the changes that so astonished Patience Kershaw did not happen all at once. Most historians agree that the Industrial Revolution occurred in at least three distinct stages.

Patience Kershaw and her family experienced the first stage of the Industrial Revolution. This stage occurred in Great Britain, North America, and Western Europe from the 1760s through the 1860s. Later the same changes took place in other countries all around the globe. During this first stage, the Industrial Revolution vastly increased the energy available to humans by developing coal-powered steam engines and putting them into factories that produced cloth.

If Patience Kershaw had lived to old age, she and her children would have seen the beginnings of the second stage of the Industrial Revolution. It started in Britain, America, and Germany in the 1860s, and it too lasted about a century. Coal power, steam engines, and cloth-producing factories remained valuable, but dramatic new technologies and products became very important. Inventors found ways to make stronger, harder steel, which was used in everything from skyscrapers to guns. Electricity, now brought

The first subways were built in the 1800s and early 1900s. Today, many modern cities have subway or underground systems.

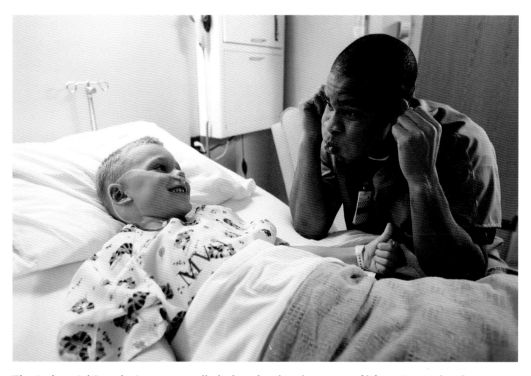

The Industrial Revolution eventually led to the development of lifesaving technologies and medicines.

under human control, was used to power factories, light up homes and streets, drive railroads and subways, and operate household appliances. Path-breaking discoveries in chemistry and biology created whole new industries: turning petroleum into gasoline (which was used to power automobiles and airplanes), producing packaged foods, creating plastics and man-made fabrics, and introducing thousands of other things that would have astonished Patience Kershaw.

Cell phone use became widespread in the 1990s, changing our patterns of communication.

We have now entered the third stage of the Industrial Revolution (also called the "Information Age"), which most historians think began around 1980. This stage is characterized by groundbreaking methods of communication in the form of satellites, cell phones, social media—not to mention music, movies, and video games! In the new economy now emerging in developed nations, heavy industry is becoming less important. In fact, many of those older industries (and the environmental problems that go with them) are now moving to Latin America, Asia, and Africa. More and more jobs in the United States, Western Europe, and Japan now involve computers and **biotechnology**.

> ### Vocabulary
>
> **biotechnology**, n. the use of living things, such as cells and bacteria, to make useful products

The Role of Capitalism

Capitalism has played a very important role in each of these three stages. Industrialists need money to open factories. Scientists and inventors need money to develop and market their discoveries. That's where investors come in. They are willing to risk their money on an idea or product that they think people will want to buy. They do this to make a profit, yet everyone may eventually benefit. One of the good things about capitalism is that it allows people to pursue private wealth while also creating things that improve the lives of other people.

What's more, because capitalists are competing against one another, there is a built-in motivation for them to make the best and cheapest televisions or dishwashers they possibly can. Otherwise, some other capitalist may put them out of business!

In order to stay in business, many capitalists and industrialists have followed Adam Smith's principles of division of labor. Division of labor has made it possible to create machines of amazing complexity. It would be fantastically difficult, perhaps even impossible, for any one person to manufacture all of the parts that go into a computer or a car. But when thousands of people create separate parts and take on separate tasks, even very large jobs become manageable.

Investors play a key role in capitalism. Nowadays, to be an investor you need only to buy some **shares of stock** in a company that makes or does something. If the company makes a profit, your shares of stock will increase in value. If the company doesn't make a profit, your shares will lose value. That's the risk you run as an investor!

Vocabulary

"shares of stock," (phrase) a small piece of a company; when investors buy shares (parts) of stock, they own a part of the company

People can spend their money on investing in companies if they choose to.

In short, capitalism has helped bring many benefits. Because of industrialism and capitalism, modern Americans are surrounded by labor-saving gadgets and luxury items that would make the kings and queens of old wild with envy.

Unsolved Problems

There's no denying that capitalism has achieved a great deal, but there's also no denying that it has created new problems and made some old problems worse. You read about some of these problems. They include child labor, health hazards, inequality of wealth, business cycles, depressions, pollution, overcrowded cities, slums, increased crime, monotonous work, and discouraged workers.

It was problems like these that led many thoughtful people in the 1800s to advocate new political and economic systems. Socialist reformers like Robert Owen wanted to help workers live better lives, while Karl Marx thought that only a revolution in which workers rose up against owners could solve the problem and create a perfect society – a communist society.

Communism has not worked out so well in practice. In most so-called communist societies, dictators govern and workers have very little say over their lives and well-being. They do not have the lives that Karl Marx imagined. Socialist utopias, such as Robert Owen's New Harmony, tended to be short-lived. The reforms imagined by many thinkers of the 1800s have not always worked out as they envisioned.

A Compromise Solution

The United States has never had a communist revolution or a socialist government. But we have not preserved capitalism in the pure form that Adam Smith described, either. What one finds in the United States (and in almost all other industrialized nations) is a sort of compromise solution. We still have a capitalist system in which people are allowed to own property and start businesses in the hopes of making money. But we have borrowed a number of ideas as well.

Here in the United States, the government is a lot more involved with the economy than Adam Smith thought government should be. The government regulates banks and businesses. It requires employers to pay a minimum wage and to provide a safe workplace. It makes laws to prevent **monopolies**, limit pollution, and prevent the destruction of the environment. There is also a **welfare system** designed to help the poor and disadvantaged. The government helps the poor by providing child care, low-cost housing, food stamps, and medical care. The elderly are protected by the **Social Security** system, which

> ### Vocabulary
>
> **monopoly,** n. complete ownership or control of a resource or industry
>
> **"welfare system,"** (phrase) a series of government programs that help poor or unemployed people meet their basic needs, such as food and housing
>
> **Social Security,** n. a U.S. government program that provides income to people who are retired or disabled

pays a pension to retired people, and Medicare, which provides health insurance. Workers are protected from some of the pains of unemployment by a government insurance system.

The idea is to combine the best aspects of all systems. How well is it working? Well, that depends on whom you ask. Some people will tell you the current system works pretty well. Others will tell you we need to get rid of a lot of welfare programs, shrink the government, and move closer to pure capitalism. Still other people will say that the government needs to place *more* limits on capitalists and do *more* to protect the poor and disadvantaged and that even today, reform is needed.

So what we do about that? Democracy depends on the involvement of citizens, so we participate in the political process. For example, almost all American adults have the right to vote. Voting for a candidate who shares your beliefs, whether it's for more government protection or stricter trade agreements, is one way to make your voice heard—and it's important to do so!

Generally, people vote for political candidates who most represent their own views.

Citizens have other ways of making their voices heard, as well. You can write to your government leaders, asking for change. You can participate in protests or demonstrations. You can join organizations that work toward the change you want to see. You can even run for political office.

Democracy is yet another thing that would probably surprise Patience Kershaw. If you told Patience that people like her could grow up to vote for the leaders of the government or even become a government leader herself, she might not believe you. "Oh, how things have changed!" she might say.

That is the story of industrialism and the Industrial Revolution. But it is not a complete story. Not every part of the story has been told, nor has the story ended. The contribution of women and of enslaved workers was incredibly significant. And then there is the issue of the environment. Over time, the Industrial Revolution affected Earth's environment in a number of harmful ways. Today we are more aware of the harmful consequences of pollution, heavy manufacturing, the removal of forests, and of intensive mining.

The Industrial Revolution is still changing the world. Indeed, the world is changing so rapidly, that, if we could travel forward 150 years in time, we would probably be just as astonished, amazed, and confused as Patience Kershaw would be if she had the opportunity to visit our world today!

As for the story itself, perhaps what you have read here will inspire you to find out more!

Glossary

A

atomic energy, n. energy that is created by splitting an atom; also called nuclear energy **(86)**

B

barge, n. a boat with a flat bottom, usually used for carrying goods **(29)**

biotechnology, n. the use of living things, such as cells and bacteria, to make useful products **(90)**

bourgeoisie, n. the upper or wealthy middle class; the people who owned the means of production, or what Karl Marx called "the haves" **(80)**

C

capitalism, n. an economic system in which resources and businesses are privately owned and prices are not controlled by the government **(38)**

capitalist, n. a person who participates in capitalism; a person who sells goods, services, or who invests money in a business **(38)**

civil rights, n. the rights that all citizens are supposed to have **(46)**

commerce, n. the buying and selling of goods and services; trade **(43)**

communist, adj. relating to communism, an economic system based on community ownership of property and industry **(76)**

confiscate, v. to take away; to seize **(82)**

D

"debtors' prison," (phrase) a jail for people who could not pay money that they owed **(50)**

division of labor, n. the breakdown of work into specific tasks performed by different people; often considered a way to make workers more efficient **(48)**

"draft animal," (phrase) an animal used for pulling heavy loads **(22)**

dues, n. money paid to an organization to become a member of that organization **(64)**

E

economics, n. the study of the management of money and resources to produce, buy, and sell goods and services **(46)**

economy, n. the way a country manages its money and resources to produce, buy, and sell goods and services **(9)**

export, v. to send goods to sell in another country **(40)**

F

free market, n. an economic system based on competition between private businesses, where the government does not control prices **(10)**

G

gentry, n. people who own land and have high social standing but no titles of nobility **(14)**

I

impersonal, adj. having no connection to people; lacking feeling **(75)**

import, v. to bring goods into one country from another country **(40)**

Industrial Revolution, n. a period of history during which the use of machines to produce goods changed society and the economy **(4)**

industrialism, n. the organization of society around an economy based on the use of machines and factories **(62)**

industrialization, n. a shift to the widespread use of machines and factories to produce goods **(4)**

inflation, n. a rise in prices and a fall in the purchasing value of money **(74)**

investor, n. a person who puts money into a business with the goal of later making a profit **(74)**

L

laissez-faire, n. a philosophy that calls for very little or no government involvement in the economy **(47)**

landlord, n. a person who owns property that other people pay to use or live in **(14)**

loom, n. a machine used to weave threads into cloth **(2)**

Luddite, n. in the early 1800s, a person who protested against industrialization by destroying machines and factories; today, the word refers to someone who is opposed to new ideas or technologies **(60)**

M

malnutrition, n. a state of poor health due to not having enough healthy food **(17)**

mercantilism, n. an economic system that aims to increase a country's wealth and power by controlling trade and people **(39)**

migration, n. the act of moving from one place to another to live **(29)**

monopoly, n. complete ownership or control of a resource or industry **(93)**

N

nutrition, n. the process of eating the right kinds of food to be healthy **(35)**

P

plague, n. a highly contagious, usually fatal, disease that affects large numbers of people **(28)**

poach, v. to hunt or fish illegally **(16)**

politics, n. the activities of leaders running a government **(55)**

poorhouse, n. a place where poor people were sent to live if they were unable to pay their bills **(8)**

prime minister, n. the head of government in some countries **(53)**

productivity, n. the rate at which goods are made or work is completed **(22)**

proletarian, n. a worker **(76)**

propaganda, n. false or exaggerated information that is spread to encourage belief in a certain person or idea **(81)**

R

raw material, n. something that can be used to make or create a product; for example, cotton is a raw material used to make fabric **(41)**

regulate, v. to control or place limits on **(70)**

S

sanitation, n. the system of keeping a place clean and free of disease **(35)**

serf, n. a peasant who is not free; a person living on a feudal estate who was required to work for the lord of the manor **(14)**

serfdom, n. an agricultural system in which people (serfs) were not free, but were required to stay and work for a landowner as the owner demanded **(14)**

shaft, n. a deep, narrow tunnel that gives access to a mine **(23)**

"shares of stock," (phrase) a small piece of a company; when investors buy shares (parts) of stock, they own a part of the company **(91)**

slum, n. a crowded city neighborhood where buildings are in bad condition; often used to refer to areas where poor people live **(35)**

social democracy, n. a system of representative government that uses elements of capitalism and socialism to govern the economy **(70)**

Social Security, n. a U.S. government program that provides income to people who are retired or disabled **(93)**

socialism, n. an economic system in which major industries are owned or regulated by the government, rather than by private businesses **(69)**

strike, n. a temporary work stoppage organized by workers as a protest **(65)**

supply and demand, n. the amount of goods and services available to buy compared with the amount that people want to buy **(47)**

T

totalitarian, adj. controlling all aspects of life **(84)**

U

union, n. an organization formed by workers to win and protect workers' rights **(9)**

utopian, adj. idealistic; usually describes beliefs about the perfect society **(70)**

W

waterwheel, n. a wheel that is turned by flowing water and used to power machinery **(22)**

"welfare system," (phrase) a series of government programs that help poor or unemployed people meet their basic needs, such as food and housing **(93)**

Y

yeoman, n. a person who owns and works on a small farm **(14)**

CKHG™

Core Knowledge HISTORY AND GEOGRAPHY™

Series Editor-In-Chief

E.D. Hirsch, Jr.

Editorial Directors

Linda Bevilacqua and Rosie McCormick

Subject Matter Expert

William Van Norman, Ph.D., Department of History, James Madison University

Illustration and Photo Credits

A Pit Head, c.1775–1825 (oil on canvas), English School, (19th century)/Walker Art Gallery, National Museums Liverpool/Bridgeman Images: 24

Add 18855 September: harvesting, ploughing and sowing, from a Book of Hours, c.1540 (vellum), Bening, Simon (c.1483–1561)/Victoria & Albert Museum, London, UK/Bridgeman Images: 17

Advertisement for Hill Bros. Millinery Goods with an interior view of the main saleroom (colour litho), American School, (19th century)/Collection of the New-York Historical Society, USA/Bridgeman Images: 72–73

Agriculture in the Middle Ages (colour litho), English School, (20th century) / Private Collection / © Look and Learn / Bridgeman Images: 16

Array of political pamphlets/Communist Party HQ, London, UK/Bridgeman Images: 85

Battle over the barricades on Alexanderplatz during the 1848 Revolutions, Berlin, 18th-19th March 1848 (colour litho), German School, (19th century) / Private Collection / © SZ Photo / Sammlung Megele / Bridgeman Images: 75

Bird's Eye View of One of the New Communities at New Harmony (litho), American School, (19th century) / Collection of the New-York Historical Society, USA / Bridgeman Images: 69

Bristol Docks and Quay, c.1760 (oil on canvas), English School, (18th century)/Bristol Museum and Art Gallery, UK/Bridgeman Images: 40

Carding, drawing and roving cotton. Carding engine (left) delivers cotton in a single sliver. Factory operated by shafts & belting. Could be powered by water or steam. Engraving c1830./Universal History Archive/UIG/Bridgeman Images: 62

Child and woman labour in the coal mines prior to 1843, drawn from contemporary prints, illustration from 'The Church of England: A History for the People' by H.D.M. Spence-Jones, pub. c.1910 (litho) (later colouration), English School, (19th century) (after)/Private Collection/The Stapleton Collection/Bridgeman Images: Cover C, 8

Coal Riddling workshop, at the mines of Blanzy, c.1860 (w/c), Bonhomme, Ignace Francois (1809–81)/CNAM, Conservatoire National des Arts et Metiers, Paris/Archives Charmet/Bridgeman Images: i, iii, 5

Cotton factory floor, showing workers mule spinning, engraved by James Tingle (fl.1830–60) c.1830 (litho), Allom, Thomas (1804–72) (after)/Private Collection/Photo © Ken Welsh/Bridgeman Images: 31

Engels (photogravure), German Photographer, (19th century)/Private Collection/The Stapleton Collection/Bridgeman Images: 77

Factory Chimneys, Howat, Andrew (20th Century)/Private Collection/© Look and Learn/Bridgeman Images: 28

H -D Falkenstein/imageBROKER/SuperStock: 7

Hargreaves' Spinning-Jenny (engraving), English School, (19th century)/Private Collection/© Look and Learn/Bridgeman Images: Cover B, 30

ICP/age fotostock/SuperStock: 90

Ingemar Edfalk/Blend Images/SuperStock: 94

Karl Marx (photogravure), German Photographer, (19th century)/Private Collection/The Stapleton Collection/Bridgeman Images: 77

Medieval Village (colour litho), Escott, Dan (1928–87)/Private Collection/© Look and Learn/Bridgeman Images: 15

Naval and Military Club, 1896 (gouache on paper), Cutler, Cecil (fl.1891–93)/Private Collection/Bridgeman Images: 55

New Lanark Mills, Scotland. Robert Owen's (1771–1858) model community of cotton mills, housing, education, world's first day nursery, evening classes, village shop (beginning of Co-operative movement). Aquatint c1815/Universal History Archive/UIG/Bridgeman Images: 68

Oliver Asks for More, illustration for 'Character Sketches from Dickens' compiled by B.W. Matz, 1924 (colour litho), Copping, Harold (1863–1932)/Private Collection/Bridgeman Images: 52

Pantheon/SuperStock: Cover A, 82

Peace with Honour - Queen Victoria (1819–1901) with Benjamin Disraeli (1804–81) following the signing of the Berlin Treaty in 1878 (oil on canvas), Wirgman, Theodore Blake (1848–1925)/The FORBES Magazine Collection, New York/Bridgeman Images: 54

Peasant Family at Table, from the Room of Rustic Scenes, in the Foresteria (Guesthouse) 1757 (fresco), Tiepolo, Giandomenico (Giovanni Domenico) (1727–1804)/Villa Valmarana ai Nani, Vicenza, Italy/© Luca Sassi/Bridgeman Images: 21

Portrait of Charles Dickens (1812–70) c.1860, Glasgow, Alexander (fl.1859–84)/Private Collection/Photo © Philip Mould Ltd, London/Bridgeman Images: 51

Radius/SuperStock: 45

Richard Levine/age fotostock/SuperStock: 92

Robert Owen (oil on canvas), English School, (19th century)/Private Collection/Bridgeman Images: 67

Roy 2 B VII f.78 Reaping corn harvest in August, from the Queen Mary Psalter, c.1310–20 (vellum), English School, (14th century)/British Library, London, UK/© British Library Board. All Rights Reserved/Bridgeman Images: 12–13

RubberBall/SuperStock: 89A, 89B

Shoe Factory (engraving) (b/w photo), English School, (19th century)/Private Collection/Bridgeman Images: 1, 49

Sir Thomas Lombe's Silk Mill, Derby, 18th century (print), Anonymous/Private Collection/Bridgeman Images: Cover D, 2–3

skeeze/Pixabay: 26–27

Strike, 1895 (oil on canvas), Munkacsy, Mihaly (1844–1900)/Hungarian National Gallery, Budapest, Hungary/Bridgeman Images: 81

Swiss peasant family (engraving), English School, (19th century)/Private Collection/© Look and Learn/Bridgeman Images: 19

The Brickyards of England, Children carrying the clay, 1871 (engraving) (b/w photo), English School, (19th century)/Bibliotheque des Arts Decoratifs, Paris, France/Archives Charmet/Bridgeman Images: 10

The Chateau de Chantilly, view of the English Garden, 1845 (oil on canvas), Barbier, Nicolas-Alexandre (1789–1864)/Musee Conde, Chantilly, France/Bridgeman Images: 78–79

The Cotton Gin, from Scenes on a Cotton Plantation, 1867 (wood engraving), Waud, Alfred Rudolph (1828–91) (after)/Boston Athenaeum, USA/Bridgeman Images: 32

The High Street from the West Bow, Edinburgh (watercolour), Rayner, Louise Ingram (1832–1924)/The Drambuie Collection, Edinburgh, Scotland/Bridgeman Images: 35

The Inauguration, plate 1 of 'The Great Industrial Exhibition of 1851', engraved by the artist, 1851 (colour litho), Nash, Joseph (1809–78)/Coram in the care of the Foundling Museum, London/Bridgeman Images: 59

The Industrial Revolution, Lampitt, Ronald (Ron) (1906–88)/Private Collection/© Look and Learn/Bridgeman Images: 25

The Mill, 1751 (oil on canvas), Boucher, Francois (1703–70)/Louvre, Paris, France/Bridgeman Images: 22

The Strike (Pittsburgh, 1877), 1886 (oil on canvas), Koehler, Robert (1850–1917)/Deutsches Historisches Museum, Berlin, Germany/© DHM/Bridgeman Images: 64

Three generations of women. Cottager spinning wool using simple wheel without treadle while her mother reels yarn and her daughter stirs cast iron pot standing on open fire No stairs, upper floor reached by ladder (left). Flagstone floor, casement windows fitted with leaded lights with diamond panes. From George Walker The Costume of Yorkshire, Leeds, 1814. Aquatint. / Universal History Archive/UIG / Bridgeman Images: 30

Title page of 'New View of Society'/British Library, London, UK/© British Library Board. All Rights Reserved/Bridgeman Images: 71

Title page, 'The Wealth of Nations' by Adam Smith, 1776 (print with handwritten annotation), English School, (18th century)/The University of St. Andrews, Scotland, UK/Bridgeman Images: 46

United States. Picking cotton. Engraving. Color./Photo © Tarker/Bridgeman Images: 32

View of Industrial Sheffield (colour litho) from the South East by William Ibbit, 1854, English School, (19th century)/Sheffield Galleries and Museums Trust, UK/Photo © Museums Sheffield/Bridgeman Images: 36–37

Wentworth Street - Whitechapel, from 'London, a Pilgrimage', written by William Blanchard Jerrold (1826–84) & engraved by A. Bertrand, pub. 1872 (engraving), Dore, Gustave (1832–83)/Private Collection/The Stapleton Collection/Bridgeman Images: 57

Westend61/SuperStock: 86–87

Workmen take out their anger on the machines, Doughty, C.L. (1913–85)/Private Collection/© Look and Learn/Bridgeman Images: 60–61